Yellow

Daniel Nunn

www.raintreepublishers.co.uk
Visit our website to find out
more information about
Raintree books.

To order:
☎ Phone 0845 6044371
🖨 Fax +44 (0) 1865 312263
💻 Email myorders@raintreepublishers.co.uk

Customers from outside the UK please telephone +44 1865 312262

Raintree is an imprint of Capstone Global Library Limited, a
company incorporated in England and Wales having its registered
office at 7 Pilgrim Street, London, EC4V 6LB – Registered company
number: 6695582

Edited by Dan Nunn, Rebecca Rissman, and Catherine Veitch
Designed by Joanna Hinton-Malivoire
Picture research by Ruth Blair
Originated by Capstone Global Library Ltd.
Production by Victoria Fitzgerald
Printed in China by South China Printing Company Ltd

ISBN 978 1 406 22599 0
15 14 13 12 11
10 9 8 7 6 5 4 3 2 1

British Library Cataloguing in Publication Data
Nunn, Daniel.
Yellow. – (Colours All Around Us)
535.6-dc22

Acknowledgements
We would like to thank the following for permission to reproduce
photographs:iStockphoto p. 11 (© Libor Tomáštík); Shutterstock p.
4 (© Petrenko Andriy), 5 (© Loskutnikov, © zmkstudio, © Richard
Griffin, © Karkas, © schankz, © WitthayaP, © marrio31, © Aleksandr
Bryliaev), 7 (© Stanislaw Tokarski), 8 (© Denis Tabler), 13 (©
piyato), 15 (© photolinc), 16 (© J Freeman), 17 (© naluwan), 19
(© Subbotina Anna), 21 (© rkucharek), 20 (© Lasse Kristensen), 22
L (© S.M.), 22 R (© Vibrant Image Studio), 23 (© Nordling), 23 (©
crystalfoto), 23 (© Dragana Francuski Tolimir), 23 (© photokup).

Front cover photograph of ducklings reproduced with permission
of iStockphoto (© Olena Mykhaylova). Back cover photographs
reproduced with permission of Shutterstock (© marrio31, ©
WitthayaP, © schankz, © Richard Griffin).

Every effort has been made to contact copyright holders of any
material reproduced in this book. Any omissions will be rectified in
subsequent printings if notice is given to the publisher.

Disclaimer
All the Internet addresses (URLs) given in this book were valid at
the time of going to press. However, due to the dynamic nature
of the Internet, some addresses may have changed, or sites may
have changed or ceased to exist since publication. While the
author and publisher regret any inconvenience this may cause
readers, no responsibility for any such changes can be accepted
by either the author or the publisher.

Contents

Yellow all around us

Let's look for colours.
It's time to play!

How many yellow things
can you find today?

Let's go for a walk

Let's go for a walk.
We won't go far.

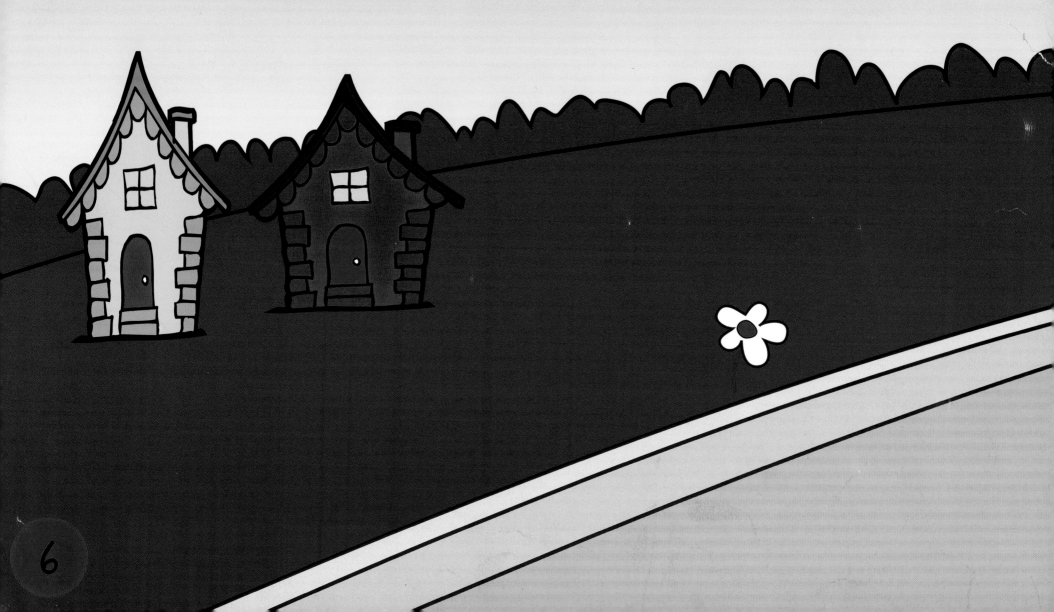

Quick, look over there!
A bright yellow car!

beep, beep!

7

Four yellow ducklings,
quack, quack, quack, quack.

All following their mum,
And looking for a snack.

Caught out in the rain?
No need to cry!

These yellow wellies
will keep your feet dry.

The sun's come out.
At last it's sunny.

Yellow sunflowers can be great fun!

They turn their heads towards
the sun.

15

Time to go home

Feeling hungry? It's time to eat!

Yellow bananas are a tasty treat.

Mmm, delicious!

17

Try yellow ice cream.
It's really yummy!

It will soon end up
inside your tummy.

18

19

Time for a bath

Splish, splash! It's time for a bath.

These yellow rubber ducks
will make you laugh.

splish,
splash

21

What else is yellow?

It has been a busy day!

Can you think of anything else that is yellow?

23

Colour challenge

Can you find four fluffy babies following their mum in this book?

Index

24